Copyright ©1998, 2002, 2014 Tho
Milford, CT 06461

All rights reserved; no part of this publication may be reproduced, stored in a retrieval system, or transmitted, in any form, without the prior written permission of Thomas C. Mercaldo

Printed in the United States.
First Printing.

Aquinas Scout Books
C/O Thomas C. Mercaldo
154 Herbert Street
Milford, CT 06461

Girl Skits contains some content that was previously published in Scout Skits, More Scout Skits, Run-ons and Even More Scout Skits and Campfire Skits

Scout Fun Books can be purchased on a wholesale basis for resale in Camp Stores, Scout Shops and Trading Posts. For details write to us at the above address or contact us by email at boyscoutbooks@aol.com. For individual orders go to scoutfunbooks.webs.com.

How to use this book

Listed at the beginning of each skit are the number of participants required and any props which may be needed. Generally, there is a minimum number needed to perform each skit, however, additional participants can usually be added. The dialog between participants is in plain text, while instructions for actors are listed in italics. Variations, when they exist, follow each skit.

Preface

During my many years in working with youth organizations, I have had the opportunity to participate in many group activities. The performance of a new skit can be the highlight of any group activity. Leaders can use this book to mentor girls through working in groups. Girls like to perform skits, and these skits can be a valuable tool in helping them gain self-confidence. Skits help youth learn to perform in front of a group. Unfortunately, it seems the same skits seem to be performed over and over again because these girls don't have exposure to ideas for new skits. Youth Skits for Girls is designed to introduce to these youth the formula for performing a huge variety of entertaining skits.

I sincerely hope that you enjoy Girl Skits, and that it helps you create outstanding group activities.

Tom Mercaldo

Table of Contents

North by Northwest 8
Walk the Plank 9
Painter's Canvas 9
I Don't Know How 10
Is it Time Yet? 11
Rough Riders 11
Campfire Beverages 12
Dying of Thirst 12
The Fortune Teller 13
Mmm Good 13
The Four Seasons 14
Sock Exchange 14
Gathering of the Nuts 15
Socks 16
Lobster Tails 16
There's a Fly in My Soup 17
Listen! 17
Panther Tracks 18
The Trained Fleas 18
Suckers on the Line 19
Covered Wagon 20
A Day at Summer Camp 21
Fire Safety Officer 22
The Restaurant 22
The World's Greatest Spitter 23

Saint Peter 24

The Little Lost Sheep 24

Thar's A Bear 25

The Important Meeting 26

The Firing Squad 26

The Secret Papers 27

Telephone Magic 27

Down South Pickin' Cotton 29

The Incredible Enlarging Machine 29

Doctor, Doctor! 30

J. C. Penney 31

The Lawn Mower 31

The Lost Lollipop 32

Oh-Wa Ta-Foo Li-Am 33

Death Scene 33

Lincoln Memorial 34

Incredible Odds 34

Letters from Home 35

The Fisherman 35

The Trained Elephant 36

Green Side Up 36

Peculiarity 37

The Rescuers 37

The Lost Neckerchief Slide 37

Reporter's First Scoop 38

Jail Thugs 38

Leaky Submarine 39

Slow Motion Theft 39
Peanuts 40
The World's Ugliest Woman 40
Sticky Gum 41
Did You Sneeze? 41
Gravity Check 42
Good for Nothing 42
The Pickpockets 42
Latrine Miscommunication 43
Football Superstar 43
Crossing the Delaware 44
The Invisible Bench 44
The Vampire Skit 45
Running Deer 45
Dragon Breath 46
Uncoordinated Actions 46
The Loon Hunt 47
Hat and Candle Skit 48
Sixty Seconds 49
The Peanut Butter Skit 49
Face Freezing 50
Telephone Answering Skit 50
Granny's Candy Store 51
The Tates Compass 51
Hardware Store 52
Submarine Training 52
Sound in the Wilderness 53

The Infantry is Coming 53
Pass the Pepper 54
Don't Brush them on me! 54
The Dead Body 55
Eat that Food 55
Tag You're It 56
The Announcement 56
Morning Coffee 57
The Echo (American Style) 57
I'm Leaving 57
The Echo 58
The Bucket Angler 58
The Vending Machine 59
The Lighthouse 60
The Siberian Chicken Farmer 61
The Complaining Monk 62
The Bee Sting 62
Gold Appraiser 63
The Queen's Raisins 63
The Rabbit Skit 64
The Cancer Sketch 64
It's All Around Me 65
Future Astronauts 65
Campfire Conference 65
The Blanket Tossing Team 66
Magic Chair 67
You Don't Say 67

The Commercial 68

Emergency Broadcast System 68

The Human Xylophone 69

The Crying Skit 69

The Viper 70

Forty-Nine 70

The Poison Spring 71

The Lost Quarter 71

The Factory Guard 72

Scientific Genius 73

Animal Impressions 73

North by Northwest

Participants: 4 minimum
Props: None

A group of girls sit along the side of the stage and a movie director approaches them. She is casting a new film and she needs someone to act as a stand in. She asks this group of girls if anyone would like to volunteer. One girl excitedly jumps up and down yelling, choose me, choose me. The director makes a concerted effort to choose someone else. she pretends not to notice this girl and tries to look past them for other volunteers. The other girls appear disinterested and finally, very reluctantly, the director chooses the enthusiastic girl.

The director next explains the part to the girl who was selected as the "Stand-in". The dialog follows:

Director: Okay now, your part is very simple. You barge in with important news for the captain. You say to her, "Captain, Captain, our ship is sinking, we've hit an iceberg." When the captain asks you how far from land we are, you tell her five nautical miles. Finally, when she asks you what direction we're headed, answer north by northwest. Do you have it?
Stand-in: Yeah, yeah, yeah, I've got it.
Director: Okay everyone take your positions .....Action.
Stand-in: Captain, Captain, your ship is stinking.
Director: Cut, cut, cut. No, no, no, your line is captain, captain your ship is sinking; sinking, got it?
Stand-in: Yeah, yeah, yeah, I've got it.
Director: Okay, action.
Stand-in: Captain, Captain, your ship is sinking. We've hit an ice cube.
Director: Cut, cut, cut. No, no, you idiot we've hit an iceberg. That's an ICEBERG. Do you think you have it?
Stand-in: Yeah, yeah, yeah, I've got it.
Director: Okay, action.
Stand-in: Captain, Captain, your ship is sinking. We've hit an iceberg.
Captain: How far off land are we?
Stand-in: Five naked models.

Director: Cuuuttttt! Its five nautical miles, not five naked models. And your next line is "North by Northwest" Do you think you can remember your lines this time?
Stand-in: Yeah, yeah, yeah, I've got it.
Director: Okay, action.
Stand-in: Captain, Captain, your ship is sinking. We've hit an iceberg.
Captain: How far off land are we?
Stand-in: Five nautical miles.
Captain: What direction are we headed?
Stand-in: Straight down.
Director: CCUUUTTTTTTT. *Director chases stand-in off stage. The end.*

Walk the Plank

Participants: 3 to 7
Props: A board and optionally pirate garb

The skit begins with the captain of a pirate ship saying "Today, someone is going to walk the plank." Other girls in the area pretend to be completing chores associated with working on a ship (swabbing the deck, raising sails, etc.). The Captain approaches each of the other girls telling them that today they need to walk the plank. Each shudders in fear and then comes up with a silly reason why they can't walk the plank today. The captain accepts these excuses by saying "Well all right" and then approaches the next girl in the group. Finally the captain approaches the last girl and says, "You're going to walk the plank." The final girl says, "OK, and she walks to the side of the stage and returns pulling a board on a rope." She is "walking the plank."

Painter's Canvas

Participants: 3 to 5
Props: Several drawings or paintings

This skit takes place at an art show. Several snooty art critics are examining the canvas's that are displayed. They are very critical until they come to one canvas which they believe is "A brilliant work of art," "Sheer genius," "An exquisite beauty," etc. They choose this canvas for a prize and call up the winning artist. The painter exclaims, "Oh my gosh! That got in by mistake. That's the canvas I use to clean my brushes!"

I Don't Know How

Participants: 4 or 5
Props: None

A group of girls (usually four) are standing in line, one behind the other. Messages are passed up and down the line with the captain, who is first issuing the commands, and the last girl answering each command with, "I don't know how."

Captain: Fire torpedo one.
Girl 2: Fire torpedo one.
Girl 3: Fire torpedo one.
Girl 4: I don't know how.
Girl 3: She doesn't know how.
Girl 2: She doesn't know how.
Girl 1: Push de button.
Girl 2: Push de button.
Girl 3: Push de button.
Girl 4: *pretends to push a button*
Captain: Missed! Fire torpedo two.
Girl 2: Fire torpedo two.
Girl 3: Fire torpedo two.
Girl 4: I don't know how.
Girl 3: She doesn't know how.
Girl 2: She doesn't know how.
Girl 1: Push de button.
Girl 2: Push de button.
Girl 3: Push de button.
Girl 4: *pretends to push a button*

This routine is done a third time. Finally, the Captain says, if we miss this time we're all going to kill ourselves.

Captain: Missed! Fire torpedo four.
Girl 2: Fire torpedo four.
Girl 3: Fire torpedo four.
Girl 4: I don't know how.
Girl 3: She doesn't know how.
Girl 2: She doesn't know how.
Girl 1: Push de button.
Girl 2: Push de button.
Girl 3: Push de button.

Girl 4: *pretends to push a button.*
Captain: Missed! *Captain shoots herself.*
Girl 2: *picks up gun and shoots herself.*
Girl 3: *picks up gun and shoots herself.*
Girl 4: *picks up gun and says,* I don't know how.

Is it Time Yet?

Participants: 4 to 5
Props: A wrist watch

To perform this skit, a group of 4 or 5 girls sit on a bench or log with their legs crossed, right leg over left. The person at the left end of the log turns to her right and asks the question, "Is it time yet?" The person to her right responds, "I don't know," and turns to her right and asks, "Is it time yet?" This is repeated until the question reaches the end person who looks at her watch and responds, "Not yet." The first person then once again asks the question and the process is repeated a second time. On the third pass the final person in the chain replies, "Yep, it's time," and together the girls lower their right legs and re-cross their legs with the left leg now on top.

Rough Riders

Participants: 5 to 7
Props: Sleeping bags

Two girls are laying on sleeping bags, one is in a tent, the other just outside it. A group of bikers come by and say, "Hey, let's beat up on this girl in the sleeping bag." Upset by this incident the girl in the sleeping bag wakes up her friend in the tent and tells her what happened. The girl in the tent dismisses the story, explaining that the whole thing must have been a bad dream. The girl in the tent commands the other to go back to sleep. A few minutes later the bikers come back and again beat on the girl sleeping outside. After they leave, she arouses her friend who again tells her it was just a dream. However, to make her feel safer they agree to change places. The bikers come back a third time and the skit ends with one of the bikers saying, "This girl's had enough, let's get the one in the tent this time."

Beverages

Participants: 4
Props: A large pot and 3 coffee mugs

Girl 1: *(Walks up to the pot, dips in her coffee mug and brings it up to her lips for a sip)*
This campfire coffee is terrible.
Girl 2: *(Walks up to the pot, dips in her coffee mug and brings it up to her lips for a sip).*
This campfire tea is terrible.
Girl 3: *(Walks up to the pot, dips in her coffee mug and brings it up to her lips for a sip).*
This campfire hot chocolate is terrible.
Girl 4: *(Walks up to the pot, dips in her hands and takes out a pair of wet socks, she wrings them out as she says:).*
I thought this would get them clean.

You can follow this skit up with a brief one-liner
Girl 1: This coffee tastes like mud.
Girl 2: That's funny, it was just ground this morning.

Dying of Thirst

Participants: 3
Props: Glass of Water and a comb

An empty glass of water is placed in the center of the stage. A girl crawls along the floor crying for water. she dies dramatically before reaching the glass. A second girl acts the same way and dies after getting a little closer to the glass than the first. A third girl comes along acting very much like the first two. This girl struggles dramatically and gets to the point just in front of the glass. At that point, she reaches into her pocket, grabs a comb, sticks it in the glass of water, combs her hair, sighs with relief and casually exits the stage.

The Fortune Teller

Participants: 5 plus 1 volunteer
Props: 3 dollar bills

MC: I'd now like to introduce the amazing Beth who can tell your fortune simply by smelling your shoe.
Beth: Thank you, Thank you. Who would like to be my first volunteer. *(Beth selects a "plant" from the audience, a girl comes forward takes off her shoe and hands it to Beth. Beth smells the shoe and predicts that a woman will give her a dollar. A nearby woman walks over and hands her a dollar.)*
Participant 1: Wow! Thanks a lot.
Beth: Who will be my next volunteer? *(Beth selects a "plant" from the audience, a girl comes forward takes off her shoe and hands it to Beth. Beth smells the shoe and predicts that a woman will give her two dollars. A nearby leader walks over and hands her two dollars).*
Participant 2: Wow! Thanks a lot.
Beth: Who will be my next volunteer? *(This time Beth selects an unsuspecting victim. The victim takes off her shoe and hands it to Beth. Beth throws the shoe to the back of the audience and says)*
I predict you will go for a long walk.

Mmm Good

Participants: 4
Props: A large pot and several spoons. A mop makes this skit more effective.

Announcer: The following skit takes places in the dining hall.
Girl 1: This sure is good soup.
Girl 2: Yeah, this is the best food we've had at camp all week.
Cook: *(carrying mop)* What are you two doing? Get those spoons out of my mop water.

The Four Seasons

Participants: 3 plus 2 volunteers
Props: none

The narrator begins by asking four volunteers to participate. Each volunteer is assigned a role in the skit; roles include a tree, a bird, a babbling brook and the trees lifeblood, the sap. Generally two of the volunteers are "plants" who know in advance their roles as the tree and the bird. The brook and the sap are then left to follow the careful instruction of the narrator. Each of the participants acts out their assigned role. For example, the tree raises her arms to signifying leaves growing in the spring. she lowers her arms in the fall.

Narrator: To the babbling brook - you need to babble.
Brook: Babble, babble, babble....
Narrator: In the spring the leaves come out on the trees (the tree raises her arms above her head), the birds begin to sing (bird - chirp, chirp, chirp), the brook begins to babble rapidly (brook starts babbling faster), and the sap, which provides valuable nutrients to the tree, begins to run (sap starts running).

The narrator continues to describe activities throughout summer and fall, and throughout this narration, the sap's job is to continue running at various paces. In the winter, the dialog ends with a narration that goes something like this: In the winter the brook freezes and stops babbling (babbling stops). The birds are gone and the trees seem lifeless and without motion. But through it all there is still some activity, for you see, the sap keeps running.

Sock Exchange

Participants: Minimum of 4
Props: None

A group of girls march in single file. An adult announces, "I know its been a long hike, and you girls are tired. Before you set up camp, I've got some good news and some bad news to tell you. The good news is after all these weeks of hiking, leadership says you can have a change of socks." *(The girls cheer)*. "The bad news is, Jane is changing with Petra, Allie is changing with Harriet......"

Gathering of the Nuts

Participants: 1 plus volunteers
Props: None

Version 1

Announcer: Andre, the famous French impressionist painter, is here to create a living portrait of nature's beauty at tonight's campfire.

(It helps to have Andre portrayed by someone flamboyant, with an overdone French accent).

Anna: Thank you, thank you very much everyone. To create this portrait I will need help from you, our lovely audience. First I will need some trees *(volunteers come forward and are positioned as trees)*. Next, I will need some birds *(volunteer birds are instructed to flap their wings among the trees)*. Eventually, hopping bunnies and a babbling brook are added with volunteers acting out these roles. Anna then turns to the audience and speaks. Another magnificent masterpiece is completed, I call this portrait, "The Gathering of the Nuts."

Version 2

Participants: No limit
Props: None

For this skit, the MC announces that the "Squirrel Patrol" will be performing the next skit. Members from the patrol walk around the crowd and select volunteers to help them with their skit. The volunteers are brought to the front of the campfire and members of the Squirrel Patrol sit down. The announcer comes forward and says let's give the Squirrel Patrol a big hand for that last skit which they like to call, "The Gathering of the Nuts."

Socks

Participants: 4
Props: Several pairs of socks

An adult drops a pile of socks on the ground and invites three girls to come up and take some.

Girl 1: I need three pair.
Adult: How come?
Girl 1: I only do laundry every three days.
Adult: Okay, here you go.

Girl 2: I need seven pair.
Adult: Seven pair? Why?
Girl 2: One for Monday, one for Tuesday, Wednesday, Thursday, Friday, Saturday and Sunday.
Adult: Okay, here you go.

Girl 3: I need twelve pair.
Adult: Twelve pair, that's ridiculous. What do you need twelve pair for?
Girl 3: *(Counting on Fingers)*
Well there's January, February, March...

Lobster Tails

Participants: 3
Props: A plate and a book

Three girls are needed for this skit. Two girls walk into a restaurant and a waiter comes in to take their order. "I'll have a steak," the first person says, and the second person orders a lobster tail. The waiter returns with one plate and a book. she gives the plate to the first person, then sits next to the second and begins to read. "Once upon a time there was a little lobster....."

This skit can be worked into a set of restaurant sketches which can include lines from the **Fly in My Soup** section.

There's a Fly in My Soup

Participants: 2 minimum
Props: None

For this skit to be effective you really need to keep it moving. This skit can be done alone or it can be worked into a series of restaurant skits which might include **Lobster Tails** or **Mmm Good**.

Patron: Do you serve crab?
Waiter: Sit down, we serve anyone.
Patron: Waiter, there's a fly in my soup.
Waiter: Quiet or everyone will want one.
Patron: What's this fly doing in my soup?
Waiter: It looks like he's doing the backstroke.
Patron: Waiter there's a fly in my soup.
Waiter: It's the rotting meat that attracts them.
Patron: What's this fly doing in my soup?
Waiter: Playing water polo.
Patron: Waiter, there's a fly in my soup.
Waiter: What's the big deal. It won't eat much.
Patron: What's this fly doing in my alphabet soup.
Waiter: Learning to read.
Patron: This food isn't fit for a pig.
Waiter: Sorry I'll bring you some that is.

Listen!

Participants: 2
Props: None

A girl sits at the center of the stage with her ear to the ground, listening intently. Another girl walks on stage watching the first girl. After a minute he, too, places her ear to the ground and listens intently. Finally, the second girl says, "I don't hear anything." The first girl replies, "I know, it's been like this all day."

Panther Tracks

Participants: 2
Props: None

Girl 1: *(pointing)* Hey look! Animal tracks. I wonder what kind they are?
Girl 2: They are obviously cat tracks. BIIGGG cat tracks.
Girl 1: You think they're from a mountain lion?
Girl 2: I don't know. Let's take a closer look.
   Both girls get on their knees
Girl 1: Well, what do you think?
Girl 2: There's no doubt about it. Those are panther tracks.
Girl 1: Panther tracks? How can you be so sure?
Girl 2: Do you see the bottom of this track. There is an ant squished at the bottom. And there's one in this track too. The animal that made these tracks was purposely stepping on ants as she walked.
Girl 1: O.K., I'll grant you this animal likes to squish ants, but how can you be so sure this cat is a panther?
Girl 2: Why that's easy. *(pointing to the ground as she talks)* Just look at the pattern. DEAD-ANT, DEAD-ANT, DEAD-ANT, DEAD-ANT, DEAD-ANT *(Say this to the tune of the pink panther theme)*.

The Trained Fleas

Participants: 2
Props: None

A person acts as a flea trainer and comes forward and explains the various tricks her flea Herman is performing. After several tricks, Herman jumps into the audience. An audience member comes forward claiming to have a flea in her hair. The flea trainer examines the audience member's head and says, "That's not Herman!"

Suckers on the Line

This skit has no less than 20 variations, here are three of the more popular versions.

Version 1

Participants: 2 plus 3 volunteers
Props: None

Girl 1: *(Pretends to dial a phone, then makes ringing sound)*
Girl 2: *(Pretends to pick up phone)* Hello.
Girl 1: Jill is that you?
Girl 2: I can hardly hear you.

Girl 2 asks for a volunteer to hold up the phone line. The same type of dialog continues until three or more volunteers are brought forward. The final dialog goes something like this.

Girl 2: Well, that's better. Now I can hear you.
Girl 1: So Jill, what have you been up to?
Girl 2: I went fishing today.
Girl 1: No kidding. Any luck.
Girl 2: Yeah, I caught three suckers on the line!

Version 2

Participants: 2 plus 2 volunteers
Props: A pole and a blanket

A candy store owner enters carrying a long pole and a blanket. She asks two volunteers from the audience to hold the pole, and then she drapes the blanket over it, explaining that inside is her candy store. A customer comes in and asks for every conceivable type of candy. The owner explains that she is out of that kind. Exasperated, the customer finally says, "Well then, what do you have?" The owner pulls off the blanket and replies, "Just two suckers on a stick."

Version 3

Participants: 2 plus unlimited volunteers
Props: A rope

Two girls walk on stage with a long rope stretched between them. One of the girls explains that she is a fisherman, the other explains that she runs the local fish market. They attempt to contact each other by phone, and the fisherman acts as if she can't hear the fish market manager. Volunteers are brought forward to hold the rope. When several volunteers are up holding the rope they can finally hear each other. The fisherman says that she doesn't have any salmon, but she did catch a bunch of suckers on the line.

Covered Wagon

Participants: 2 plus volunteers
Props: None

One girl acts as a covered wagon; she is positioned at the front of the audience on her hands and knees. The other girl is the wagon driver. The wagon driver uses the following monologue:

Darn, my wagon wheel is broken. I need a volunteer to hold it on the wagon. *(The driver selects a volunteer who stands next to one of the wagon wheels)*

Darn it this wagon still won't go. Now the other wheel is loose. I need another volunteer to hold this wheel on the wagon. *(The driver selects another volunteer who stands next on the other side of the "wagon").*

There that did it. Now it will work. All I needed was a couple of nuts to hold on the wheels.

A Day at Summer Camp

Participants: 4 minimum
Props: Sleeping Bags, a bag of M & M's, a deck of cards

This skit features a narrator and two girls. The narrator reads a sugary story about what life at summer camp is like. The girls then act out the complete opposite of what the narrator says. The narrator's piece follows in plain text, examples of what the girls might do follow in italics.

Narrator: "You jump out of bed to the excitement of another day at camp." *The girls slowly get out of their sleeping bags and say, "Oh no not another rainy day."*
Narrator: "The cook sounds off, "Come and get it", and you enjoy a hot hearty breakfast."
The girls open up a bag of M & M's and begin eating.
Narrator: "After breakfast there's work to be done, you tidily re-organize your tent," girl*s roll their sleeping bags into a big mess,* "and help clean up the camp area." girl*s throw the empty bag of M & M's and other trash from their tent on the ground.*
Narrator: "You're now ready for the day's adventure. What will it be today? A hike along a wilderness trail? Knot tying sessions? Exploring a cave, canoeing or swimming?"
One of the girls says, "Do you want to play poker?" and they sit down to play cards.
Narrator: "So much to do, yet so little time. Afternoon at camp has a way of rocketing by. So many things to do, so little time."
Girl *says, "I'm bored, there's nothing to do here." A second girl says, "You could sit here and watch me play solitaire. The second girl does.*
Narrator: "There's the archery range, you could build a signal tower, or go for another swim. Supper is probably the eating highlight of the day. But at camp it is even much more than that, it is a chance for girls to share in good fellowship. *A fight breaks out among the girls.*
Narrator: Hurry now! Supper's over and it's time to enjoy the campfire. *The girls slowly walk to the campfire.*
Narrator: "There's fun galore as you gaze into the campfire and feel the strong bonds of comradeship that's pulling you and your friends together."
One girl pushes another away from her.
Narrator: "After the campfire the girls return to their tents. Happy dreams! Tomorrow is another day full of excitement and surprises."

Fire Safety Officer

Participants: 2
Props: A bucket of water. Optional: raincoat or firemen's gear

The campfire begins with the MC introducing the Fire Safety Officer. The Fire Safety Officer comes out holding a bucket of water as the MC discusses the importance of having water near a fire. The Fire Safety Officer's only job is to make sure that the campfire does not get out of control. The more serious the MC can be in portraying the danger of fire, the better this routine works. If the Fire Safety Officer can wear a raincoat, firemen's suit or uniform, it will make her easier to identify later in the evening. The Fire Safety Officer goes over and stands to the side and the MC goes on with the program.

Later in the program victims are selected to assist in a variety of skits. **The Firing Squad** skit is performed and when someone yells fire, the Fire Safety Officer runs over and throws water on the firing squad. During **I Don't Know How or Leaky Submarine**, the Fire Safety Officer can douse the girl who says "Fire torpedo one." **Dying of Thirst** can be performed and when the girl crawls on the ground crying water, the Fire Safety Officer runs out and throws water on the crawling girl. Needless to say the Fire Safety Officer can have a busy night running out and throwing water every time she hears the "keywords" fire or water.

The Restaurant

Participants: 2 minimum plus volunteers
Props: Glasses of water

The narrator initiates this skit by asking for a volunteer. This volunteer is instructed to get on her hands and knees to serve as a bar or table. Next, additional volunteers are asked to act as customers at a restaurant. The customers are instructed to sit next to the table and they are told to converse while the waiter offers them a drink. The waiter then places two water glasses on the table, (the back of the first volunteer) while the customers are chatting. The skit ends when the customers are told the restaurant is closed, and it is time to leave. The "table" is left with the job of trying to get up without spilling water on her back.

The World's Greatest Spitter

Participants: 3 minimum
Props: A bucket of water

This skit requires several girls, a spitter, a catcher and some "plants" who remain in the audience. A bucket half filled with water is left on stage.

A participant, the spitter, walks on stage and proclaims that she is the greatest spitter in the world. she brags about her ability, and claims that she can spit farther than any other living being. "Plants" in the audience challenge the spitter to prove it, saying they do not believe her.

The spitter agrees to take up the challenge and asks for a volunteer to assist her. She selects the "catcher" who acts as if she expects to be the victim.

The spitter explains that she will stand 10 feet away from the catcher, and that she will spit directly into the bucket, demonstrating her distance and accuracy. The catcher complains saying, "You'd better not hit me with your spit!" "You just need to make sure you hold the bucket still, "the spitter replies.

The spitter **pretends** to spit and the catcher pretends to catch the spit tapping the bottom of the bucket as if the spit made noise as it hit the can." The spitter hams it up and takes a huge bow.

The "plants" in the audience act unimpressed claiming "Anyone could do that." So the spitter responds by repeating her feat from several distances. At last the spitter claims she will prove she is the greatest by spitting completely around the world. she pretends to perform that feat and takes an even bigger bow.

The "plants" complain that the spitter is a fake and they yell for her to get off the stage. They say no one could spit around the world. The spitter says that she can prove that she did it. With that she says to the catcher, "Show them."

The Catcher then throws the bucket of water on the crowd.

Saint Peter

Participants: 4
Props: None

A girl is introduced as Saint Peter who is guarding the pearly gates to heaven. A group of three girls arrive at the pearly gates each hoping to get into heaven.

Girl 1: Saint Peter can I go into heaven?
Saint Peter: First you need to tell me how you suffered on earth.
Girl 1: I went on a long hike and got blisters on my feet.
Saint Peter: I'm sorry, you haven't suffered enough, you can't enter.
       (Girl 1 walks away, disappointed)
Girl 2: Saint Peter can I go into heaven?
Saint Peter: Tell me how you suffered on earth.
Girl 2: I spent a week eating camp food.
Saint Peter: I'm sorry, you haven't suffered enough, you can't enter.
       (Girl 2 walks away, disappointed)
Girl 3: Saint Peter can I go into heaven?
Saint Peter: How did you suffer?.
Girl 3: I was in (pick the name of someone with a sense of humor) (campsite, friends, family, etc.)
Saint Peter: Welcome to Heaven!!!

The Little Lost Sheep

Participants: 4 minimum
Props: None

The MC introduces what is arguably the top singing camp in the United States. Their many awards include the Fulbright songster award and the Alto choir prize. After a big build up, the patrol marches forward as the MC announces their number, "The Lost Little Sheep." On the count of three the camp sings one word "Baaaa-aaa-aa-a".

Thar's A Bear

Participants: 2 plus volunteers
Props: None

The skit leader selects several volunteers from the audience who are told to mimic the actions of the skit leader. It may be beneficial to have the second person be in on the skit so that each subsequent person knows what to do. However, you can just spring this trick on several unsuspecting victims, if you explain it well enough. The volunteers line up side by side facing the audience. The skit leader begins, then pairs of girls in the line repeat the following dialog and actions. The skit leader purposely mispronounces her words; volunteers are instructed to mimic the skit leaders pronunciation. Mispronunciation is important, it adds a great deal to the skit.

Skit leader: There's a Bar (Bear).
Girl 1: Whar? (Where?).
Skit leader: Over Thar (There)
Skit leader points her right arm across her body and remains in this position.
Girl 1: Over Thar? (There?)
Skit leader: Over Thar (There)
Girl 1: There's a Bar (Bear).
Girl 2: Whar? (Where?).
Girl 1: Over Thar (There)
Girl 1 maintains her action pointing her right arm across her body.
Girl 2: Over Thar? (There?)
Girl 2 points her right arm across her body and remains in this position.
Girl 1: Over Thar (There).

Girl 2 and girl 3 repeat this exchange, girl 3 and girl 4, etc., until all volunteers are standing with one arm pointed across their body. The Skit leader starts again, this time pointing with the left arm across her body, while maintaining the action of pointing her right arm across her body. The dialog and actions are repeated all the way down the line. Next the Skit leader lifts her right leg and points it to the left and again all girls follow her action while continuing to hold their crossed arms pointed in opposite directions. One final time the Skit leader begins, this time pointing her head left toward the bear, with all the volunteers following suit. At this point all the volunteers have reached the point of being quite silly, and quite off balance as each is standing on one leg with arms crossed and head tilted. The skit leader then pushes the first girl in the line and the entire group will fall over like dominoes. You have no idea how funny this skit can be until you've seen it performed.

The Important Meeting

Participants: 4 minimum
Props: Toy microphone (optional)

The important meeting skit can incorporate up to 10 girls. Additionally, you can use this skit to introduce shy girls to participating in skits without requiring them to take a major role. The skit begins with some number of girls seated around a table in a serious discussion. Some girls may be taking notes, others may be pretending to be in passionate and animated discussions. A narrator speaks over the committee and introduces herself as a television reporter. In hushed tones the narrator talks about these individuals coming together to help make some very important decisions.

The narrator completes her role by saying something like "let's listen in and hear what these committee members have to say." The group quiets down and a committee chairman stands up and says in a loud voice, "Then it's decided. We'll have two large pizzas, one with pepperoni, the other with sausage."

The committee members cheer in agreement.

The Firing Squad

Participants: Minimum of 6
Props: Toy rifles or sticks are optional

A firing squad lines up as if to shoot a prisoner. Just as the time comes the prisoner yells, "Earthquake!", and the firing squad runs off, allowing the prisoner to escape. Another prisoner is brought forward, and this one escapes after yelling, "Tornado." This can be repeated with earthquake, avalanche, etc. The final person is brought out having seen the others and she attempts to do the same thing. Just as the firing squad is getting ready, this person yells "Fire", and the firing squad does.

The Secret Papers

Participants: 4 minimum
Props: None

This Skit can also be done as the special papers, royal papers or the important papers. The main idea is that some person of authority, who in this example we will call the Queen, calls in her assistants and tells them that she urgently needs the secret papers. Different assistants return one at a time with various papers (newspapers, pamphlets etc.)Which the person of authority discards. As each assistant returns with the wrong "secret papers" the Queen becomes more and more agitated, demanding in stronger and stronger terms that her less than intelligent assistants bring her her secret papers. The skit concludes when an assistant supplies the Queen with a roll of toilet paper and this assistant is praised by the Queen who then scurries off the edge of the stage.

Variations:
Substitute the president or a business executive for the Queen.
Have the assistant who supplies the secret papers be a court jester who is knighted for supplying the secret papers.
Have each servant who does not get the correct secret papers executed for their incompetence.

Telephone Magic

Participants: 4 minimum
Props: Banana, neckerchief, an old cap, a cup, eggs and a magic wand

All props are placed on a table in the front of the room. The MC comes forward and announces that tonight's magic show has to be canceled because the magician cannot make it. A phone rings and the MC pretends to be in a conversation with the magician who is off stage. The magician has agreed to have a volunteer from the audience perform her tricks by following her telephone instructions. The MC selects a volunteer who is really a "Plant" who is part of the act. The volunteer comes forward and acts like she does not understand the directions. she picks up the phone and begins to follow the magician's instructions which are audible to the entire group.

Magician: Take the neckerchief from the table.
Volunteer: Duh, aaahh, which one is the neckerchief?
Magician: You know, it's like a handkerchief.
Volunteer: Hinkerchiff?
Magician: What are you some kind of fool? Handkerchief, it's like a bandanna.
Volunteer: Banana, why didn't you say so. I've got it right here.
Volunteer picks up the banana.
Magician: Okay, take the bandanna and fold it in half.
Volunteer: Okay.
   Volunteer breaks the banana in half.
Magician: Now make a fist and stuff the bandanna in your fist.
Volunteer: *Volunteer stuffs the banana in her fist.*
Magician: Now say the magic words, "Abra ca dabra", and the bandanna will be gone.
Volunteer: Da Crabra
   Volunteer opens her fist to reveal a soggy banana.
Magician: For our next trick grab the cup.
Volunteer: Okay, I've got the cap.
Magician: Break two eggs into the cup.
Volunteer: *Volunteer breaks some number of eggs in the cap but miscounts Like 1, 4, 2.*
Magician: Now beat the eggs with the magic fork.
   Volunteer strikes the cap several times with the fork like you would beat someone with a club.
Magician: Now place the magic hat on your head.
   Volunteer places the hat on her head as eggs drips onto her face.
Magician: Now wave the magic wand over the cup and say the magic words, abra ca dabra. Turn the cup over and it will be empty.
   The empty cup is turned over.

The MC says let's give a big round of applause for our volunteer. she then reminds girls not to be too quick to volunteer during skits or they can end up with egg on their face.

Down South Pickin' Cotton

Participants: 4
Props: Boom box, jacket, sneakers and a towel

Girl 1 is standing in the middle of the stage as several other girls walk by one at a time.

A girl walks by carrying a boom box
Girl 1: Hey where did you get that great stereo?
Girl 2: Down south pickin' cotton.
   A girl walks by wearing a jacket
Girl 1: Where'd you get that great jacket?
Girl 3: Down south pickin' cotton.
   A girl walks by wearing sneakers
Girl 1: Where'd you get those cool sneakers?
Girl 3: Down south pickin' cotton.
   A girl walks by limping, and beat up wearing nothing but a towel.
Girl 1: What happened to you?
Girl 4: I'm Cotton.

The Incredible Enlarging Machine

Participants: 2 plus multiple volunteers
Props: Backdrop, bucket of water and large and small objects

This skit requires small and large versions of objects. If you didn't bring props on your campout, you can always use small and large version of pots, rope, logs etc. Set up a large backdrop using a sheet, sleeping bag or blanket. A girl hides behind this blanket with the large props and a bucket of water. The narrator is in front of the blanket with the small objects.

Narrator: I have developed the world's first enlarging machine. I can take any object and make it bigger. I will need a few volunteers to help me demonstrate how the machine works.

Volunteers are called forward. The Narrator hands them small objects and they throw them behind the blanket. Larger versions are tossed out by the hidden girl. The last volunteer is the victim. The Narrator hands the victim a cup filled with water. She whispers in the victim's ear that there is really a girl behind the blanket and the trick is to walk to the edge of the blanket and to douse the girl behind the curtain with the cup of water. As the victim does this, the girl behind the curtain douses the victim with a bucket of water.

Doctor, Doctor!
Participants: 2 minimum
Props: None
For this skit to be effective you really need to keep it moving. This can be done by having a series of girls walking on stage back to back as doctor and patient. Or the skit can be done by the same two girls appearing quickly between each skit.

Patient: Doctor, I'm scared. This is my first operation.
Doctor: I know just how you feel. You're my first patient.
Patient: Doctor, do you think I'll kick the bucket?
Doctor: No, but you do look a little pail.
Patient: Seriously Doctor, am I going to die.
Doctor: That's the last thing you'll do.
Patient: Doctor, doctor, everyone says I'm a bell.
Doctor: Take two aspirins and give me a ring in the morning.
Patient: Doctor, can I sleep in my contact lenses?
Doctor: No, your feet would stick out.
Patient: Doctor, doctor, I feel like a set of drapes.
Doctor: Pull yourself together.
Patient: Doctor, doctor, I feel like a pack of cards
Doctor: Quiet, I'll deal with you later.
Patient: Doctor, doctor, everyone keeps ignoring me.
Doctor: Next!
Patient: Doctor, do you think that raw oysters are healthy?
Doctor: I never met one that was sick.
Patient: Doctor, you've got to help me. I keep thinking I'm invisible.
Doctor: Who said that?
Patient: Doctor, doctor, I'm afraid I'm a Kleptomaniac.
Doctor: Are you taking anything for it?
Patient: Doctor, doctor, I think I'm suffering from amnesia.
Doctor: How long have you had it?
Patient: Had what?
Doctor: You've got too much snew growing on your arms.
Patient: What's snew?
Doctor: Not much, what's new with you?

J. C. Penney

Participants: 4
Props: A pair of jeans, a jacket, sneakers and a towel

Girl1 is standing in the middle of the stage as several other girls walk by one at a time.

A girl walks by wearing jeans.
Girl 1: Hey, where did you get those great jeans?
Girl 2: J. C. Penney.
A girl walks by wearing a jacket.
Girl 1: Where'd you get that great jacket?
Girl 3: J. C. Penney.
A girl walks by wearing sneakers.
Girl 1: Where'd you get those cool sneakers?
Girl 3: J. C. Penney.
A girl walks by wearing nothing but a towel.
Girl 1: Who are you?
Girl 4: J. C. Penney.

Variations
This skit can also be done as L. L. Bean or Montgomery Ward.

The Lawn Mower

Participants: 2 plus volunteers
Props: None

Participant 1 serves as the announcer, a second participant acts like a lawn mower. Participant 1 pretends to pull the string in order to start the mower. The mower (Participant 2) sputters, but refuses to start. The first Participant then calls for volunteers to try and start the mower. The final volunteer successful starts the mower, and the announcer says, "I guess all it took to start the mower was a big jerk.

The Lost Lollipop

Participants: 2
Props: A blanket

This skit requires 2 girls, one plays the part of a girl who has lost her lollipop, the other plays the role of a monk from an eastern religion. Optionally, the monk can be dressed in a blanket, symbolizing a monk's robes.

Girl: *Sobbing* I've lost my yummy little red lollipop.
Monk: *Walks in with hands together chanting ummmm...he stops and asks*: What's the matter my girl?
Girl: Weren't you listening? I've lost my yummy little red lollipop.
Monk: Well, have you looked for it?
Girl: I've looked and I've looked, but I just can't seem to find my yummy little red lollipop.
Monk: When your eyes fail you, you must reach for a higher consciousness. If you chant loud enough, the location of your yummy little red lollipop will be revealed to you.
Girl: Chant?
Monk: Yes, chant. Just keep repeating the phrase, my yummy little red lollipop, my yummy little red lollipop.....
Girl: My yummy little red lollipop, my yummy little red lollipop, my yummy little red lollipop..... it's not working.
Monk: Perhaps you chant too softly. (*Turning to the audience*) Maybe you can help. Just repeat after me. My yummy little red lollipop, my yummy little red lollipop.....(*The monk gets the whole audience loudly repeating the phrase. she then turns back to the girl.*) Did it work?
Girl: (*Very loudly*) No, but I did find a whole lot of suckers!

Oh-Wa Ta-Foo Li-Am

Participants: No limit
Props: None

In many campsites, this routine was reserved for introducing new girls to campfires. Since this skit cannot be performed on the same person twice, it should be used only occasionally, at small settings. Participants are called forward and are told to kneel in front of the campfire. Next, they are instructed to raise their arms above their head. In a repetitive motion they should touch the ground in front of them with their hands and then raise them above their heads again. This action fans the fire, and the fire god likes it a lot. While acting in this way, girls must repeat the fire god's words of worship, Oh-Wa Ta-Foo Li-am. These words should be repeated slowly at first, with the words in each successive chant faster and closer together. When a person becomes enlightened to the meaning of the fire god's words, they are instructed to whisper the meaning to the MC. The MC tells the girls who understand the phrase to sit down. Hopefully before too long all of the participants will understand that they are repeating, "Oh What a Fool I am."

Variations:
Other phrases such as: Oh-Wa Ta-Gu Si-Am, or Oh-Wa Ta-Nas Si-Am may be used instead.

Death Scene

Participants: 3 minimum
Props: None

A girl who is a real over-actor plays the part of a soldier who has been fatally wounded and is about to die. She is not wearing dog tags so the medics cannot identify the soldier. Repeatedly they ask her name and the soldier responds by crying phrases like help, water, medic, etc. Finally, the medic tells the soldier that she is about to die and they need to know her name so they can tell her mother. The soldier finally speaks her first sentence, "My mother already knows my name!"

Lincoln Memorial

Participants: 3
Props: A container

A girl sits motionless while an announcer and a Doctor stand beside the girl:

Announcer: We are standing here at the Lincoln Memorial where Dr. Van Guildersmith is about to test her latest invention which transforms calcium into living tissue. She hopes to bring Abraham Lincoln back to life so we can gain some valuable insight into the thinking of this tremendously popular man.
The Doctor pretends to pour the substance on the girl who is acting as the statue. The statue moves and begins to speak.

Statue: Four Score and Seven Years ago...
Doctor: Mr. Lincoln, Mr. Lincoln.
Statue: Where am I?
Doctor: I have brought you back to life so you could share with us your incredible insight.
Statue: I see.
Doctor: Let me begin by asking you if there was one thing you wished you had done when you were alive what would it be?
Statue: Well, I wish I had used my gun more.
Doctor: Used your gun more? Mr. Lincoln, I thought you were a man of peace.
Statue: I am, but if I had it to do all over again I would have killed every pigeon within 500 miles of Washington.

Incredible Odds

Participants: 3 minimum
Props: None

A small group of girls come out onto the stage (for this example we'll use 3) looking like they've just been in a terrible fight. They converse using language like, "What a fight, what a battle, we should never have taken them on in the first place, 3 against 100, in the face of incredible odds," etc. The performers should really build the situation up. Finally, the skit ends when one person says, "You know those were the toughest three kids I've ever seen."

Letters from Home

Participants: 2
Props: 2 sheets of paper

It helps to have each person write their script on a piece of paper. They can read from the script, and pretend to be reading from the letters.

Girl 1: Hey, I got a letter from home!
Girl 2: So did I! What does your letter say?
Girl 1: Well, my sister says her doctor told her she needs to work out with dumbbells. She wants to know if I can exercise with her when I get home.
Girl 2: My Mom says she is writing this letter very slowly, because she knows I can't read fast.
Girl 1: My dad got a new job with 500 men working under him. He's cutting grass at the cemetery.
Girl 2: My dad lost his job delivering flowers. Apparently he was afraid to go into girls' houses. His doctor said he was a classic example of a petrified florist.
Girl 1: Our neighbors started keeping pigs. My Dad got wind of it this morning.
Girl 2: My sister had a baby. She doesn't say if it's a boy or girl, so I'm not sure if I'm an Aunt or an Uncle.
Girl 1: Oh, there's a PS, it says I was going to send you $10.00, but I already sealed the envelope.
Girl 2: Throw me some paper so I can write back.
Girl 1: I can't toss it if it's stationary.

The Fisherman

Participants: 4 minimum
Props: Sticks, string and worms

A group of girls sit in a line holding sticks with string hanging from them. They pretend to cast, and all the girls but one, complain about how they are not catching anything. The one "quiet" girl pretends to reel one fish in after another. Finally one of the girls asks the successful fisherman what her secret is. The fisherman mumbles an unintelligible response. No one understands what she said so they ask again, "What's you're secret to catching so many fish?" Finally, the successfully fisherman spits worms into her hands and replies, "You have to keep the worms warm."

The Trained Elephant
(Dimbo the Elephant)

Participants: 3 plus volunteers
Props: A poncho and a canteen

An announcer and two additional girls perform in this skit. Two girls walk together with a poncho draped over them. The front person swings her arm back and forth like an elephant swings her trunk. The person in the back carries a canteen filled with water (The canteen is hidden under the poncho). The announcer states that she is an elephant trainer and she has trained her elephant, Dimbo, to carefully walk over girls. The announcer asks for a brave volunteer to come forward so Dimbo can demonstrate her skill. A volunteer is selected, and the volunteer lies on the ground. Dimbo slowly steps over the volunteer. Two additional volunteers are chosen, and these volunteers lie alongside the first, spaced about two feet apart. Once again Dimbo gracefully steps over each of them. Finally, the trainer announces that she would like Dimbo to have a chance to break the world record by successfully walking over 5 girls. Are there two more volunteers? Dimbo begins to walk over the volunteers and the person who is playing the back end of Dimbo pours water on each of the volunteers that are laying underfoot. The announcer ends the skit by saying it looks like Dimbo had a little accident or you can just let the volunteers jump up and return to their seats.

Green Side Up

Participants: 4 minimum
Props: None

Leader: Our camp has undertaken a project to restore this park.

The girls begin work on the project. The Leader remains at center stage. An adult approaches the leader and begins an audible dialog with her(it doesn't matter what they discuss). The leader keeps interrupting their conversation to yell to the other girls, "Green Side Up." Finally the adult speaks.

Adult: What is it you keep yelling to them?
Leader: Oh, they're putting in sod and I just want to make sure they put the correct side up this time.

Peculiarity

Participants: 2
Props: None

Girl 1: Hello, Jill.
Girl 2: Helllllooo Megan.
Girl 1: Do you always stutter.
Girl 2: Nnnnoooo. Only when I I I tallk.
Girl 1: How come you stutter?
Girl 2: It's my p-p-peculiarity. Everyone has s-some p-p-peculiarity.
Girl 1: Oh yeah. I don't.
Girl 2: D-d-don't you stir your c-c-coff-eeee with your r-r-right hand?
Girl 1: Yes.
Girl 2: See that's your p-p-peculiarity. Most people use a spoon.

The Rescuers

Participants: 3
Props: None

This skit requires three girls. One person is lying on the floor. Two others come walking in.

Girl 1: Look, this girl is badly hurt. *(Girl 1 checks her vital signs)* She's got no heartbeat. We need to do CPR. *(Girl 2 joins girl 1 on the ground and they begin CPR).*
Girl 2: One, two, three, four, five, breathe......I'm getting tired, I think we'd better switch. *(At this point, girl 3, the injured party, gets up, girl 2 lies down and they begin CPR on girl 2).*

The Lost Neckerchief Slide

Participants: 2
Props: None

Girl 1: *Searches around the campfire for a lost neckerchief slide.*

Can you help me? I've lost my neckerchief slide.
Girl 2: Do you remember where you were standing when you lost it?
Girl 1: Yes, over in that pine grove.
Girl 2: Over there?
Girl 2 points into the darkness.
Girl 1: Yea, that's the spot.
Girl 2: Then why are you looking for the slide over here?
Girl 1: Are you kidding? It's dark over there.

Reporter's First Scoop

Participants: 5
Props: None

A reporter is standing on the Brooklyn Bridge, about to jump. she is depressed because she can never get a big story ahead of the other writers in town. One by one others come along who have failed miserably in life. A teacher who hates students, a boat captain who gets seasick, a gardener with hay fever, a construction worker afraid of heights, etc. Each is depressed and each decides to jump alongside the reporter. In the end they stand at the bridge and the reporter yells one, two, three. Everyone except the reporter jumps. The reporter takes out her notebook and yells, "What a scoop!" "Four girls jump to gruesome deaths!"

Jail Thugs

Participants: 4 to 8
Props: Deck of Cards

Participants act as if they are prisoners in "jail." A guard enters the area and yells "lights out!" The participants pretend to all go to sleep, and as soon as the guard leaves they get up and begin playing cards. One participant asks all of the others what they did to get sent to jail. Each answers with a story like "I robbed a bank." participants respond favorably to each story up until you reach the last person. The last person says, "You know those tags on mattresses that say 'Do Not Remove Under Penalty of Law'? Well I cut one off." The other prisoners all scatter screaming in fear and horror.

Leaky Submarine

Participants: 3 plus 1 volunteer
Props: None

This skit begins with 3 girls walking on stage. Each person is holding a cup, one person, who is acting as the commander, is holding two cups. The commander explains that her camp is small and she needs a volunteer to help with this next skit. A volunteer is selected and placed in line between the other two girls from the camp. The Commander explains that she is in charge of the submarine and each of her assistants work in the torpedo room. She hands an empty cup to the volunteer explaining that these paper cups are torpedoes. The group is organized in a line and the commander says, "Fire torpedo one". This phrase is passed down the line until the end person throws her cup into the fire. This routine is repeated again, this time with the volunteer throwing her paper cup into the fire. As they begin the third round the commander begins to say "Fire torpedo th...", when she stops in mid-sentence and yells, "incoming torpedo, incoming torpedo." The second person on line says, "Captain, we've sprung a leak in torpedo chamber two," and throws her cup, which is filled with water, on the volunteer.

Slow Motion Theft

Participants: 3
Props: A comb, wallet, jackknife, keys, etc

Two pickpockets announce to the crowd that they will demonstrate their incredible skill at their profession. A pedestrian comes walking toward them, and the pickpockets walk up to her, quickly brush up against her and continue to walk by. When the pedestrian disappears, they show all the things they stole from her (use whatever is handy like a wallet or jackknife, be sure to show a lot of stuff).

The pickpockets then ask the audience if they would like to see in slow motion, how the theft was done. They return the stuff to the pedestrian (Make sure the pedestrian puts the stuff in pockets where it will fall out easily) and re-enact the routine walking super slowly. The pickpockets bump into the pedestrian, pick her up, turn her upside down and shake her vigorously until all the stuff falls out. The pickpockets drop her on the ground, pick up the stuff, put it in their pockets, pick up the pedestrian, set her back on her feet and all parties continue on their way.

Peanuts

Participants: 5
Props: None

The lifeguard takes a group of girls over to a camp ranger.

Lifeguard: Here's a group of trouble makers Miss.
Ranger: Don't worry, I'll take care of them.
    (Lifeguard leaves)
    Okay. Spit it out. What did you two do?
Girl 1: Nothing. I just threw peanuts into the lake.
Girl 2: It's true. All we did was throw peanuts into the lake.
Ranger: *(Turns to the third girl)* Is this true? What do you have to say for yourself?
Girl 3: I'm Peanuts Miss!

The World's Ugliest Woman

Participants: 4 plus 1 volunteer
Props: A Sheet

The master of ceremonies brings out a girl who is covered by a blanket. The MC explains that this is the world's ugliest woman. This woman is so ugly that no one can bear to look at her face without screaming and falling to the ground dead.

The master of ceremonies asks for volunteers to view the world's ugliest woman. She selects a "plant" from audience and instructs the "plant" to stand face forward behind the world's ugliest woman. The sheet is lifted so that only the volunteer can see the world's ugliest woman. The volunteer screams and falls to the ground. This continues with several more "volunteer plants" coming forward viewing, screaming and fainting. Finally, the MC picks a girl, or preferably, an adult from another camp. When the sheet is raised the world's ugliest woman screams and faints.

Sticky Gum

Participants: 4 minimum
Props: None

This is another one of those skits with lots of variations. Here's one way to perform the Sticky Gum Skit.

The skit begins with one girl on stage chewing gum. She gets called away and before she goes she sticks the gum somewhere like on a tree. After she disappears, another girl comes forward and leans against the tree into the gum. This girl shakes the gum off her hand onto the ground. This girl exits and another girl comes on stage and steps in the gum. This girl scrapes the gum off her shoes onto a park bench and then leaves. Another girl enters, sits on the bench and leans her hand into the gum. she gets up and scrapes her hand against the tree to get rid of the gum. she exits and the original girl enters the stage. she says something like, "let's see, what was I doing. Oh yeah, " and walks up to the tree, takes the gum, puts it in her mouth, starts chewing and walks offstage.

Did You Sneeze?

Participants: 4 minimum
Props: None

A line of soldiers comes marching along. The last soldier in the line sneezes, and the commander, who is first in line, turns around and asks, "Did you sneeze?" The second soldier in line responds, "No," the leader calls her a liar, and whacks her on the side of the head. The soldier falls out of line and troop continues to march.

This process continues with each soldier being whacked out of the line until all that remains is the commander and the last soldier. The soldier sneezes and the commander asks, "Did you sneeze?" The soldier responds, "Yes, mam." The commander replies, "God Bless You" and they march away.

Gravity Check

Participants: 2
Props: None

Two girls walk on stage. The first person stops suddenly and says, "Gravity check!" Both girls jump, and then the second person says, "Still working!

Good for Nothing

Participants: 2
Props: None

This skit requires a girl, and an adult who doesn't take herself too seriously.

Girl: (*walking toward the adult*) If I'm good throughout the entire camping trip will you give me $10.00?
Adult: When I was your age, I was good for nothing.

The Pickpockets

Participants: 2
Props: A comb, wallet and a pair of underwear

Two old friends meet and embrace each other. They talk about what they've been up to, and both reveal that they've become pickpockets. The first exclaims that she is by far the best pickpocket in the world. The second responds that, he, in fact, is the better pickpocket. To prove it, she reveals the comb and wallet belonging to the first pickpocket, explaining that she stole them when they embraced. The first pickpocket replies, "That's nothing, look what I took from you." The first pickpocket reveals a pair of underwear; the second pickpocket peers into her shorts to see that her underwear is missing, grabs the underwear from the first, and runs off stage.

Latrine Miscommunication

Participants: 1 plus 3 volunteers
Props: None

Three girls are selected from the audience and are taken away from the stage where they can no longer hear the announcer. The girls are told that this is a contest. They are each instructed to act out an assigned part, and they are then told that the audience will be trying to guess who or what they are. The first volunteer is told to act like a jockey; the second is told to act like a fighter plane pilot, and the third is instructed to act like a bulldozer.

At the campfire, the MC has told the audience that these three girls have been at camp all week and have been unable to use the bathroom. The audience thinks that they will be acting out their first trip to the latrine in a week. Needless to say, this miscommunication can have interesting results.

Football Superstar

Participants: 4 minimum
Props: A doll

The scene is a fire at a high rise building. One person plays the role of a mother on the third floor of the burning building, another person serves as the football superstar, the rest of the girls acts as the crowd. The mother is yelling, my baby, my baby, somebody save my baby. The football superstar comes forward and claims that she is the greatest receiver to ever play the game. Just throw the baby down from the burning building and she will surely catch it. The mother throws the baby and the crowd ooh's and ah's as the baby is drifting far from the football superstar. At the last minute the superstar catches the baby on the dead run and the crowd cheers. Then the football superstar spikes the baby into the ground.

Crossing the Delaware

Participants: 4 minimum
Props: Rowboat (optional)

If a rowboat from camp is available, it makes this skit work much more effectively. A group of girls are sitting in a rowboat. One of the girls stands in the front and plays the part of George Washington. The MC introduces this group as George Washington and her men crossing the Delaware. The MC gives this situation a big buildup, describing how tired the troops must be and suggests that everyone listen to George Washington's inspirational direction as they reach shore. As she is finishing speaking the girls sitting in the boat begin to yell, "Hooray we've reached shore." George Washington waves her arms for silence and says, "Okay everybody, get out of the boat.

The Invisible Bench

Participants: 4 minimum
Props: None

The first participant is squatting as though she were sitting on an invisible bench. A second girl comes in and begins the dialog.

Girl 2: What are you doing?
Girl 1: I'm sitting on the invisible bench.
Girl 2: Can I join you?"
Girl 1: Sure, there's plenty of room.
  Second girl pretends to sit. A third girl comes along, and the scene repeats. This can be done with as many girls as there are in the patrol. Finally the last girl comes along and asks,
Last girl: What are you doing?
Girl 1: I'm sitting on the invisible bench.
Last girl: But I moved it over there this morning!

AAAAHHHHHH!! All the seated girls fall down.

The Vampire Skit

Participants: 2
Props: None

Scene: One vampire, standing onstage, takes a can marked "blood", pours tomato juice from it into a glass and drinks it. The second vampire enters.

Vampire 1: Mmm. Delicious. Vould you like some?
Vampire 2: No, thanks. I couldn't drink another bite.
Vampire 1: So vat's new?
Vampire 2: Nothing much. I just saw a poor old bum begging on the street corner.
Vampire 1: You did. Vat did she say?
Vampire 2: She vanted me to help her. She said she hadn't had a bite in days.
Vampire 1: So what did you do?
Vampire 2: Vat else? Naturally, I bit her!

Running Deer

Participants: 2

The skit begins with a young girl addressing a Leader.

Girl: Mighty Leader, why was my brother named Running Deer?
Leader: Because on the day he was born, I saw a dear running past my teepee.
Girl: Why was my sister named Flying Eagle?
Leader: Because on the night she was born I saw a Flying Eagle.
Girl: And why was my older sister named Galloping Buffalo?
Leader: Because on the night that she was born, I saw a Galloping Buffalo. Why do you ask me so many questions, Bear Throwing Up?

Dragon Breath

Participants: 4 to 7
Props: Blanket

A girl draped in a blanket plays the part of a terrible dragon with terrible breath. Three or four "volunteers" are "planted" at various points in the audience; they are selected to come up one at a time to say hello to the dragon. Each time a person says hi to the dragon, the dragon replies, "Hello!" and the "volunteer" falls over dead (there is a lot of room for girls to ham this up). Finally, a real volunteer is selected to say hello to the dragon. When she says, "Hello, Dragon," the dragon falls over dead.

Uncoordinated Actions

Participants: 2
Props: Long sleeve shirt and a sheet or blanket

This skit can be performed in a variety of ways. The central concept of the skit is one girl performs some act while another girl who cannot be seen by the audience provides the hand motions for the girl. The girl can be an opera singer, and the hand motions can be done at inappropriate times during the song. These stray hands can cover the singer's mouth or eyes during the performance, or the singer's stomach can be rubbed or her face slapped. There is really no limit to what can be done with this skit. Here's how the skit is done:

A large button down shirt is fastened backwards around the singer/performer. The singer/performer does not place her arms in the shirtsleeves. A second individual (the uncoordinated actor) stands behind the first, placing her arms through the shirtsleeves. A sheet is placed between the singer/uncoordinated performer so that the uncoordinated performer cannot be seen (It is best to cut a sheet specially for this purpose, but this skit will work simply by draping a sheet in a position such that the head of the "uncoordinated performer" is not seen.

Variations: This skit can be performed with more than one set of singers/uncoordinated actors. Another variation involves no singing at all, performers/uncoordinated actors can simply try to perform simple acts in line with the performer's narration like making a sandwich, eating from a bowl, tying shoes, etc. There is no limit to the humorous skits that can be built off of this concept.

The Loon Hunt

Participants: 5
Props: None

Narrator: This is the story of the little-known Medicrin and two hunters' efforts to capture it. The Medicrin, which has been dancing around during the Narrator's speech, suddenly spots the two hunters, who blunderingly, and unsuccessfully, attempt to catch the Medicrin. During the next speech, all actors act according to the Narrator's storyline.
Narrator: Several times our bold hunters attempted to catch this Medicrin; they use traps, "Medicrin" calls, even a sick loon. Every once in a while the actors make appropriate comments. But all this was to no avail. Finally, they consulted a wise man.
Hunter 1: Wise woman, we have been trying to catch the Medicrin for quite a while, but without any success. We even tried to lure it with a sick loon, because we'd heard that it was a good idea. What do you suggest?
Wise Woman: Speaks in an old, strained, many years-of-experience, sage voice. You have been going about it in almost the right way. But the Medicrin also needs a sweeter trap!
Hunter 1: Bewildered Uh... Thank you, Wise man! Let's go!
Hunter 2: What did she mean by a sweeter trap?
Hunter 1: I don't know. Maybe we should feed our sick loon some sugar!
Hunter 2: Sugar?
Hunter 1: Yeah! You know, like sugar cured ham!
Narrator: And so our brave hunters took a bag of sugar and forced it down the loon's throat. Ahh ... Watch now as the Medicrin spots our loon.

The Medicrin sees the loon and DIVES for it, at which point, the hunters capture the Medicrin.

Narrator: Our brave hunters have finally succeeded in capturing the Medicrin. Which, just proves that . A loonful of sugar helps the Medicrin go down!

Hat and Candle Skit

Participants: 1 or 4
Props: Various hats and a candle

This skit is best performed by one person, although it can be done with 4 performers. A single performer uses various hats and voice intonations to indicate which character is speaking. The Mother talks in a high voice with the lower lip out and up, and wears a fancy shower hat. The Father wears a ball cap with the peak to the left side and talks out of the left side of her mouth. The educated daughter, speaks in a normal voice, and wears the ball cap to the front. The other daughter wears the cap to the right, and talks out of that side. The father and other daughter have drawls. The candle is burning, in front of the performer.

Father: Well, it is sure good having you home from college daughter. Hope you're getting a good education.
Ed Daughter: Oh I am, it won't be long and I'll graduate.
Daughter: Sure enough you won't want to be stayin' down here on the farm.
Mother: Now, Jill, Sally'll be visitin' often enough.
Father: [yawning] It's been a long day, and hearin' about all that college learnin' has made me tired. I'm goin' ta turn in.
All: [indicate agreement]
Mother: This durn'd candle's always a problem to put out, but out it's got to go. [tries to blow it out, but because of lip, air goes up] Hey Pa, I can't do it again, you try it
Father: [blows, but air goes sideways] Cain't do it neither Ma. Jill, you have a go.
Daughter: [blows, and blows, but air goes to other side] Ain't no good Pa. I try and try, but all I get is chapped lips. Jill, show us what all that educamation has done fer ya.
Ed Daughter: [licks finger and thumb, pinches out flame - exits]

Sixty Seconds

Participants: 5
Props: None

Five girls walk in a line counting quickly:

Girl 1: 1.
Girl 2: 2.
Girl 3: 3.
Girl 4: 4.
Girl 5: 5.
Girl 1: 6.
Girl 2: 7

The counting continues until girl 5 reaches the number 60. Then together they all say, "We have just wasted one minute of your time. Thank you."

The Peanut Butter Skit

Participants: 3
Props: Lunch Bag and Peanut Butter Sandwiches

Announcer: Sets the scene. It is noon, and time for lunch break at a school. Here begins Act 1.
Julia: Takes out lunch, looks into lunch bag, carefully, picks out a sandwich, unwraps it, examines it and scowls. Peanut butter! She then throws sandwich away while others watch.
Announcer: Act 2
Julia: Takes out lunch, looks into lunch bag, carefully, picks out a sandwich, unwraps it, examines it, scowls and yells Peanut Butter! hurls sandwich away while others look on, shaking their heads.
Announcer: Act 3
Julia: Repeats the actions in act 2 another student speaks
Friend: Excuse me for butting in, but I've noticed that every day you look at your sandwich and throw it away. Why don't you tell your mom you don't like Peanut Butter?
Julia: You leave my mom out of this, I make my own sandwiches!

Face Freezing

Participants: 2
Props: None

The following skit usually involves a girl and an adult.

Girl: When you were little did your parents ever tell you that if you made an ugly face for too long, your face might freeze like that?
Adult: Yes they did.
Girl: Well you can't say you weren't warned.

Telephone Answering Skit

Participants: 3
Props: None

Three girls are needed to perform this skit. They should sit far away from each other, pretending to be speaking on the phone.

Tracy: Hello, this is Tracy.
Shannon: Hello Tracy. What's up?
Tracy: I'm in Washington and I'm really broke. I need $100 right away. Can you help me out?
Shannon: What's that, Tracy? I can't hear you. Must be a bad line.
Tracy: I'll call you right back.
Ring, Ring
Shannon: Hello.
Tracy: Shannon, it's Tracy, I need to borrow $100.
Shannon: Tracy, I still can't hear what you're saying. We've got a bad connection.
Tracy: Let me get the operator to help us. Click. Hello operator can you connect me to Shannon.
Shannon: Hello.
Tracy: Shannon, it's me Tracy again, I need to borrow $100.
Shannon: still can't hear you.
Operator: Hello, this is the operator. I can hear him clearly.
Shannon: Then you give him the $100!

Granny's Candy Store

Participants: 4 performers and 6 volunteers or 7 performers and 3 volunteers
Props: None

The skit begins with the announcer saying how much she used to enjoy going to Granny's candy store. The announcer says that she is going to recreate the scene at Granny's with the help of three performers and six volunteers. One of the performers is assigned the job of being Granny while the other two are told they will be shoppers. Then six volunteers are brought forward, the first three are told to stand in a corner, while the next three are given instructions to play various parts. The first of these plays the part of a cash register (This volunteer stands up and say "Ching, Ching, Ching, repetitively), a popcorn machine, (This volunteer repeats, pop, pop, pop), and a rocking chair, (this volunteer sways back and forth saying, "Creak, Creak, Creak"). The three girls standing in the corner are given no part to play. The shoppers come in and ask Granny for various items, and to each request Granny replies, "I'm sorry dearie, I'm all out of those." Eventually the shoppers get mad and ask, "Well then, what do you have?" Granny answers by stating all she has is these three suckers standing in the corner.

The Tates Compass

Participants: 3 to 4
Props: One or several compasses

The Skit leader hands a compass one at a time to several volunteers or if she has enough compasses, she provides each volunteer with a compass. she then instructs them to find north, being especially careful to keep the compasses clear of their belt buckles. she explains how easy it can be for the compass to point at the metal in the belt rather than at the North Pole. After each successfully finds north or their assigned bearing she congratulates them and says there is one more important thing you must remember. Never use a Tates compass. When one of the participants asks why, the Skit leader replies by saying,

"You know the old saying, she who has a Tates is lost."

Hardware Store

Participants: 2
Props: None
Girl: (walks in) Have any grapes?
Clerk: No, this is a hardware store.
Girl: (walks in out then back in) Have any grapes?
Clerk: No, this is a hardware store.
Girl: (walks in out then back in) Have any grapes?
Clerk: No! If you ask for grapes one more time, I'll staple your hands to the counter.
Girl: (walks in out then back in) Have any staples?
Clerk: (relieved she didn't ask for grapes) No.
Girl: (laughs) Have any grapes?

Submarine Training

Participants: 1 plus a volunteer
Props: A cup of water, a picture of a ship, and a raincoat

Storyteller: I need a volunteer to take submarine training. (Put victim under the coat and hold up an arm of the coat to use as a periscope.) Now to be a good submarine captain, you must be able to use the periscope. So let's practice a bit. Can you see the fire? How about those tents? The table? The moon? The stars? (Continues until she becomes proficient.) Let's start our mission. You are the captain of this fine submarine, the SS Tornado. You are to bring it about on maneuvers, and sink enemy ships. So here we go, in the middle of the Atlantic Ocean. Oh! Here comes an enemy ship to the right! Can you see it? (Show a drawing of a ship.) Blow it up! (When she fires, sink the ship.) Good going! Now turn the submarine to port and then to starboard. (Make fun of the volunteer for not knowing port is left & starboard is right) Oh, there's a storm brewing. (Shake her a bit.) Do you see that island? Try to go over there to seek cover. Can you see the waves? My, aren't they big? And they're crashing against the rocks! What a big storm! Can you see it? Can you see the waves? No? (Pour the water down the arm.)

Sound in the Wilderness

Participants: 6
Props: None

Participants assume a variety of roles including storyteller, bird, frog, tree, breeze, and leader. The Storyteller is telling the story to the campfire crowd, while the other actors, with the exception of the lost leader, have the option to hide in the woods, sit in the crowd, or stand beside the storyteller. The leader must hide in the woods.

Storyteller: You know, I love camping. It's not like being in the city at all. You hear sounds that you can only hear out in the country. For example, listen to the chirping of the birds. (Bird chirps a lot, sings a bird song.) Ah, isn't that lovely? And the frogs, they have one of those great sounds. (Frog calls out ribbit sounds.) And though there can be a breeze in the city, it's just not the same as the breeze in the country. (Light breeze being called out.) Let's face it; there are trees in the city, but how many? The breeze through a forest is so nice (Light breeze, slight swishing of the trees.) But the sound I love to hear the most when I go camping is the sound of the Lost leader. (Heavy thumping of the feet; calls out, "Where in the world am I?")

The Infantry is Coming

Participants: 2 minimum
Props: Small tree

A participant runs out on stage yelling, "The infantry is coming, the infantry is coming." Later, (you can do this seconds later or after the next song or skit), a second person comes out yelling, "The infantry is coming, the infantry is coming." This happens three or four times. Finally, one or two girls come out on stage holding a small tree and they proclaim, "The infant tree is here!"

Pass the Pepper

Participants: 3 or more
Props: Toilet paper, pepper shakers (optional)

Ma: Pass the peppa, Pa.
   This message is repeated by each person in a line up to the last person, Pa, who responds:
Pa: Here's the Black Peppa, Ma.
   Goes down the line to Ma, who responds:
Ma: No, not the Black Peppa, Pa.
   Goes down the line to Pa, who responds:
Pa: Oh. Here's the Chili Peppa, Ma.
   This goes on through different kinds of Peppa i.e. Banana Peppa, Jalepeno Peppa, Red Peppa, Green Peppa, and so on until...
Ma: Can't you pass the toilet peppa, Pa?

Don't Brush them on me!

Participants: 2
Props: None

The Scene: A Psychiatrist's office. A patient is lying on the couch. The Doctor is sitting on a chair.

Doctor: Let's see, last week we were talking about your past.
Patient: Yes, I think we were.
Doctor: How much sleep do you get at night?
Patient: Oh, I can't complain. about nine hours I guess.
Doctor: Well, that seems pretty normal. I am beginning to wonder what we are going to find wrong with you. You seem just as sane as I am.
Patient: (horrified) But Doctor, it's these creepy crawly bugs. I just can't stand them! (Leaps from couch and brushes herself wildly). They're all over me, they're all over me.
Doctor: (steps back) Well for goodness sake, don't brush them onto me.

The Dead Body

Participants: 3
Props: None

A girl is lying on the ground pretending to be dead. Another walks up and finds the "Dead" girl lying on the ground. A third girl is off in the distance, acting as a police dispatcher receiving a call.

Girl 2: Hello, hello, is this the police?
Girl 3: Yes, it is.
Girl 2: I've just found a dead body at the corner of Sycamore and First Avenue.
Girl 3: Can you spell that?
Girl 2: Uh, S I K (looking around for a sign), no I mean S Y K.....wait a minute, let me drag her over to First and Elm.

Eat that Food

Participants: 3 to 5
Props: A watch, a large quantity of a food item like marshmallows or bananas

This very straightforward skit requires a large quantity of some sort of food item (marshmallows, bananas, bread, prunes or biscuits are good). The skit features a skit leader and 2 to 4 contestants. The skit leader announces that we are going to play a game called, "Eat That Food." she selects 2 to 4 contestants from the audience. The contestants are then told that the low bidder will be required to eat 10 marshmallows. Contestants then bet on how long it will take them to eat the ten marshmallows. Whoever bets lowest actually has to do it in that period of time. This skit is based on the Name That Tune game. Actual dialog would go something like this.

Skitleader: To first contestant What is your bid?
1st Contestant: I can eat ten marshmallows in thirty seconds.
2nd Contestant: I can eat that may marshmallows in twenty seconds.
3rd Contestant: I can do it in ten seconds.
Skitleader: Eat That Food.

Tag You're It

Participants: 2
Props: Distinctive clothing, a poncho, a fake mustache, a fake nose and glasses

This skit requires two girls to dress distinctively so that they are easily recognized later. The first (Girl 1) has a club and is chasing the second (Girl 2) who is running. Girl 2 runs through the audience; she hides behind the master of ceremonies, she climbs a tree, she sits in with the crowd. Girl 2 can be as creative as she desires. Girl 2 must run and girl 1 must try to grab her. They must both run out of sight without one catching the other.

Later after another skit has been performed, girl 2 comes into the fire ring panting. She asks, "Has anyone seen girl 1?" girl 2 keeps trying to hide, but girl 1 seems to find her wherever she goes. "Don't tell her where I am," girl 2 pleads with the audience. Then you hear girl 1 yelling from beyond the campfire ring, and girl 2 runs off. Girl 1 chases after her, seemingly intent on blood.

At the next interlude, girl 1 comes into the fire ring panting and carrying her club. Has anyone seen that no-good girl 2? Girl 1 is going to get her, and when she catches her he's going to give it to her good. At this point girl 2 is actually hiding in the audience, wearing a poncho, a fake mustache and glasses. Girl 1 spots her and girl 2 jumps and runs off.

At the next interlude, the duo comes crashing in again, but girl 2 trips. girl 1 towers over her, raises her club, then taps her with her other hand. "You're it!" she intones as she drops the club and runs away. Now girl 2 picks up the club and chases girl 1.

The Announcement

Participants: 2
Props: None

MC: And now it's time to make a spot announcement.
Girl: Makes the sound of a dog barking.
MC: Thank you Spot.

Morning Coffee

Participants: 2
Props: None

Leader: *to girl* "This coffee tastes like mud!"
Girl: That's funny; it was just ground this morning.

The Echo (American Style)

Participants: 2
Props: None

The skit leader announces during the singing that she has noticed an echo around the campfire and she is going to demonstrate how the echo works. The following dialogue takes place between the leader and the echo (a skit performer who is out of site).

Leader: Hello.
Echo: Hello.
Leader: Bread.
Echo: Bread.
Leader: Cheese.
Echo: Cheese.
Leader: Baloney.
Echo: (silence)
Leader: Baloney.
Echo: (silence)
Leader: (acting surprised and embarrassed) The echo must have stopped working. Let me try again. (He then says in a louder voice) This leader is great.
Echo: Baloney.

I'm Leaving

Participants: 2
Props: Garbage bag, leaves

The first girl walks across the area scattering handfuls of leaves she takes from a big bag. Another girl approaches and asks, "What are you doing?" The first girl replies, "I'm leaving!"

The Echo

Participants: 2
Props: None

One participant, "The Echo," hides in the woods behind the campfire while the other, "The girl," comes to the front of the campfire.

Girl: Girl, it's been a tough day at camp. But now I've hiked up to the famous Echo Mountain, might as well give it a try. (Raises voice) Testing …1…2… 3…
Echo: Testing.
Girl: I'm a girl and I'm trained to live in the woods, (raises voice) right!
Echo: Right!
Girl: And when it's my turn to cook, if I mess up the stew the rest of the girls can lump it, *(raises voice)* correct!
Echo: Correct!
Girl: And I'll tell that to the leader too. *(raises voice)* Check!
Echo: Check!
Girl: T*urning to hike away, in an arrogant tone* No one's gonna push me around and treat me like a JERK.
Echo: JERK! Girl *does a double take and exits.*

The Bucket Angler

Participants: 2
Props: Bucket, pole, and string

An angler sits at the front of the campfire holding a fishing pole. The end of the fishing line is sitting in a bucket as if the angler is fishing in the bucket. The angler begins to pull on the line as if she has just hooked a large fish. At this moment another girl walks past the angler, does a double-take and walks over to talk to the angler. They begin a dialogue that can go something like this:

Girl: Hey, Joe what are you doing?
Angler: I'm fishing, silly, what does it look like I'm doing?
Girl: Fishing? What are you fishing for?
Angler: I'm fishing for suckers.
Girl: Have you caught any?
Angler: Yes, as a matter of fact, you're the third today.

The Vending Machine

Participants: 2
Props: Pitcher of water, paper cups, quarters

Girl: I'm dying of thirst! Water! Water! What's this? A vending machine?
Vending Mach: DEPOSIT TWENTY-FIVE CENTS PLEASE. The vending machine is a girl holding a pitcher of water and a cup.
Girl: Twenty-five cents? Oh. Hmm. She takes a quarter out and puts it in the guy's shirt pocket.
Vending Mach: The machine holds out the glass, holds out the pitcher, and mechanically pours the water into the space right next to the glass, missing the glass and pouring on the ground. The girl desperately tries to grab the water being poured on the ground.
Girl: Water! Water!
Vending Mach: DEPOSIT TWENTY-FIVE CENTS PLEASE. The girl digs in her pockets, finds another quarter. she puts it in the machine's shirt pocket. The machine holds out the glass, holds out the pitcher, and mechanically pours the water into glass. WATER! The girl starts to take it, but before she does the machine turns the glass upside down, dumping the water on the ground. The girl scrambles for the water on the ground, but doesn't get any.
Girl: Water! How do I get water out of this stupid machine?
Vending Mach: DEPOSIT TWENTY-FIVE CENTS PLEASE. The girl digs in her pockets, finds another quarter. she puts it in the machine's shirt pocket. The machine holds out the glass, holds out the pitcher, and mechanically pours the water into the glass. Then the machine drinks it itself.
Girl: After digging in both pockets I've only got one quarter left. I better get some water this time! The girl places her last quarter in the machine's pocket, and the machine spits water in her face (the machine stored it in its cheeks when it drank the previous glass).

The Lighthouse

Participants: 7 to 11
Props: 1 or 2 flashlights

This skit requires a narrator, 3 to 5 girls and an equal number of leaders. Girls play the role of lighthouse walls. Leaders will be "recruited" from the audience to assume a "support position." The skit begins with girls standing in a circle, facing out, with their feet touching, (their feet are spread 2 – 3' apart). A single flashlight (or optionally 2 if more than four girls are used), is held at eye level and is passed around the circle. girls stand tall and hold the beacon's beam steady. The Narrator begins:

Narrator: Many years ago the girls of a seaside village built a lighthouse to warn approaching ships of a dangerous shoal near their harbor. The beacon from this lighthouse could be seen for miles, even in fog and storms. For many decades, the lighthouse stood firm and gave safe passage to all who sailed by the village. But as the years went by, the villagers grew old and so did the lighthouse. The villagers could no longer make repairs; the ocean's waves wore away the foundation. The weary lighthouse sagged and failed in its duty.

The girls now bend at the waist, with their heads leaning toward the side. They bend their knees slightly and pass the light around, shining it erratically.

Narrator: When the schooners and square riggers started to go aground on the shoals, the old villagers knew they had to call in experienced girls to help solve their problem. Girls who were pillars in their own communities and who were as solid as rock. They turned to the leadership of the adults of the group.

The Narrator now calls on some of the prestigious area leadership and instructs them to come forth and support their falling lighthouse. She instructs them to go down on their hands and knees and into holes in the walls (between the girls' legs). Leaders are facing in with their derrieres out, and are straddled by the girls who again stand tall and give a steady light.

Narrator: Now with these new rocks placed into the foundation, the lighthouse once again shines a bright beacon and stands firm in the stormy surf to withstand the pounding of the waves.
Girls drop the flashlight and then hand paddle the leaders.

The Siberian Chicken Farmer

Participants: 4
Props: None

Farmer: Here, chick chick chick … Here, chick chick … chick …
    Two military times come up behind the farmer.
Police: Comrade! Vat are you doink?
Farmer: I'm feedink my chickens.
Police: Vat are you feedink dem, Comrade?
Farmer: Corn.
Police: Fool! There is a shortage of corn!!!
    They beat her up. Oof. Ow.
Police: *dragging her away* Three years in the work camps for you!
Narrator: Three years later, …
Farmer: Here, chick chick chick … Here, chick chick … chick …
    Two military times come up behind the farmer.
Farmer: *stands up* Uh oh …
Police: Comrade! Vat are you doink?
Farmer: I'm feedink my chickens.
Police: Vat are you feedink dem, Comrade?
Farmer: Wheat.
Police: Fool! There is a shortage of wheat!!!
They beat her up. Oof. Ow.
Police: D*ragging her away* Five years in the work camps for you!
Narrator: Five years later, …
Farmer: Here, chick chick chick … Here, chick chick … chick …
Two military times come up behind the farmer.
Farmer: *stands up* Uh oh.
Police: Comrade! Vat are you doink?
Farmer: I'm feedink my chickens.
Police: Vat are you feedink them, Comrade?
Farmer: Rubles.
Police: Rubles? But vy are you feedink them rubles, Comrade?
Farmer: They can buy their own food!

The Complaining Monk

Participants: 3
Props: None

Narrator: This skit is about the monks in a monastery who are only allowed to speak two words every ten years. Our friendly monk is about to come in and say her two words, after ten long years of silence.
Abbot: *(Chants some blessing, then,)* Yes, my son, what do you wish to say?
Monk: Bad food!
Narrator: Well, ten years have gone by, and of course our friendly monk's time has come again to say her two words. she of course is not quite as young as she used to be, and walks a touch more slowly.
Abbot: *(Chants some blessing, then,)* Yes, my son, what do you wish to say?
Monk: Uncomfortable bed!
Narrator: Well, yet another ten years have gone by, and of course our friendly monk's time has come again to say her two words. she is really old at this point, having been at the monastery for thirty, long, devoted years.
Abbot: *(Chants some blessing, then,)* Yes, my son, what do you wish to say?
Monk: I quit!
Abbot: I'm not surprised! You've been here for thirty years and all you've done is complain!

The Bee Sting

Participants: 2
Props: None

Girl 1: OOOOOOUCH, OOOOOH, OOOUCH!
Girl 2: What's the matter?
Girl 1: A bee stung my thumb.
Girl 2: Try putting some ointment on it.
Girl 1: But the bee will be miles away by now.

Gold Appraiser

Participants: 4
Props: Bags filled with rocks or candy, a table

The skit begins with a gold appraiser sitting behind a table. Prospectors come in with their gold and ask the appraiser to value it.

Girl 1: (Walks in with a bag of rocks) Can you tell me what this is and how much it's worth?
Appraiser: It's Fool's Gold and it worthless.
Girl 1: What'll I do with it?
Appraiser: Leave it here, I'll take care of it.
Girl 2: (Walks in with a bag of rocks or candy and repeats the action) Can you tell me what this is?
Appraiser: It's Fool's Gold and it worthless.
Girl 1: What'll I do with it?
Appraiser: Leave it hear, I'll take care of it.
Girl 3: (A third miner walks in) What do you have there?
Appraiser: I got dem fool's gold!

The Queen's Raisins

Participants: 4 to 7
Props: None

Queen: I am the Queen. Bring me my raisins!
1st Squire: Here are raisins, sire, from the hills of California!
Queen: Those raisins are not fit for peasants! Bring me my raisins!
2nd Squire: Here are raisins, sire, from the vineyards of France!
Queen: They are hardly worth sneezing at. Bring me my raisins!
3rd Squire: These raisins, sire, were handpicked with tweezers by Benedictine **Monks** in Germany!
Queen: These raisins are NO GOOD! Bring me my royal raisin supplier!
Two squires drag in the royal raisin supplier.
Queen: Why have you not brought me my raisins?
Royal Supplier: My rabbit died!

The Rabbit Skit

Participants: 2
Props: None

Girl 1: Ask me if I'm a rabbit.
Girl 2: Okay Are you a rabbit?
Girl 1: Yes. Now ask me if I'm a beaver.
Girl 2: Are you a beaver?
Girl 1: No, silly. I already told you I was a rabbit!

The Cancer Sketch

Participants: 4
Props: Tin can (A knife , fork, salt & pepper shaker, tweezers and wrench are optional.)

Three girls surround a girl lying down.
Doctor: What seems to be the problem here?
Assistant: She has a bad case of cancer
Doctor: I see. This will be tough. Knife.
   The assistant hands the doctor a knife.
Assistant: Knife
   The doctor sticks out her hand.
Doctor: Fork.
   The assistant hands her a fork.
Assistant: Fork
Doctor: Salt and Pepper.
   The assistant hands her salt and pepper.
Assistant: Salt and pepper
Doctor: I have found the liver. Monkey wrench.
   Assistant hands the doctor a monkey wrench.
Doctor: I have found the it. Tweezers, there, that should do it.
Assistant: You have removed the can sir!

The assistant holds up an old tin can.

It's All Around Me

Participants: 2
Props: Belt

A girl runs into the room yelling, "It's all around me! It's all around me!" A second girl asks, "What's around your?" The first girl replies, "My belt."

Future Astronauts

Participants: 3 minimum
Props: None
Setting: Three girls are bragging about their futures as astronauts.

Girl 1: When I grow up, I'm going to Mars.
Girl 2: Well, I'm going to Neptune.
Girl 3: I'm going to the Sun.
(1st two girls scoff at this last statement.)
Girl 1: It's too hot on the sun.
Girl 2: Yeah, your rocket will melt.
Girl 3: What do you think I am? Stupid? I'm going at night!

Campfire Conference

Participants: 6 to 8
Props: none

Six or eight weary-looking girls enter the campfire circle, silently circling the campfire once, and then sitting in a ring around the fire. After a long pause, the first girl sighs and says, "What a day!" There's another pause for deliberation before the second girl sighs and says, "What a day!", and yet another before the third repeats, and so on around the circle until they reach the last girl. she sighs and says, "You betcha." The first girl then turns and says in disgust, "If you can't stick to the subject, I'm getting out of here!" Then she rises and leaves the campfire, followed by all the others.

The Blanket Tossing Team

Participants: 5 to 7
Props: A blanket (optional)

This takes about six girls, who form a circle around an invisible blanket, with a small invisible girl (Lynn) who sits in the middle of the invisible blanket and gets tossed.

Leader: We're an Olympic blanket tossing team, and Lynn in the middle here is our star blanket bouncer. We'll toss Lynn a bit just to warm up. One, two, three! One, two, three! One, two, three!
On three each time, the team lets the pretend blanket go slack, then pull it taut. They watch the invisible Lynn go up in the air, then come down, and they gently catch her again in the blanket. Each time they toss her higher. The team has to be in sync, and they have to watch about the same spot -- the easiest way to do this is to have everyone just imitate the leader, who is the speaker.
Leader: OK, we're all limbered up now? The team murmers in agreement. Then let's toss Lynn a bit higher. One, two, three!
Lynn comes up, and the team adjusts their position a bit to catch her as she comes down.
Leader: One, two, three!
This time wait about ten seconds, and move quite a bit to get under her. Move this way and that before finally catching her.
Leader: One, two, three!
Twenty seconds this time, almost lose track of her, adjust the position here, there, and here again.
Leader: What? What's that you say, Lynn? *pause* Audience, you are in luck! Lynn wants to go for the world record blanket toss! Ready team? One! Two! Thrreee!!! A mighty toss! *The team shifts positions, like trying to catch a high fly ball.* There she goes! She's past the trees! She's really up there! *pause, looking hard into the sky* Do you see her? I've lost her. Where'd she go? *another pause* Oh well. The team leaves the stage, and the program continues.
After another skit and song, and preferably in the middle of awards or announcements of some sort, Lynn! Quick team! *The blanket tossing team runs back on stage, positions themselves this way and that, and catches Lynn.* Let's have a big hand for Lynn! Hurrah!!!

Magic Chair

Participants: 5
Props: Two Chairs

Scene begins with doctor sitting on one of the chairs. The first patient enters twitching their left arm.

Doctor: And what's wrong with you?
Patient 1: As you can see doctor I have this terrible twitch.
Doctor: Just sit on my magic chair and you'll get better.
The patient sits on the chair and stops twitching, but the doctor's left arm starts twitching.
Patient 1: Oh thank you doctor. you cured me.
The patient leaves, the doctor still twitching calls for the next patient.
Doctor: Next......And what's wrong with you
This patient has the hiccups. The process of sitting in the chair is repeated. The doctor now has a twitch and the hiccups. The third patient is called in, both her legs keep flicking in the air. The process is again repeated so that the doctor now has a twitching arm the hiccups and both legs flicking in the air. The doctor now calls patient four. This patient looks quite normal, enters and sits in the magic chair.
Doctor: And what may I ask is wrong with you Miss?
Patient 4: I've got a terrible case of the runs doc.
The doctor runs off the stage holding her stomach.

You Don't Say

Participants: 2
Props: Phone

Girl 1: (pretends to answer a phone) Hello? Yes? You don't say ... You don't say ... You don't say ... You don't say? ... You don't say! ... You don't say. Bye!
Girl 2: Say, who was on the phone?
Girl1: She didn't say!

The Commercial

Participants: 3 or more
Props: None

Director: Okay, girls! Let's get going!
Cameraman: But Miss!
Director: No interruptions! Action!
Actor: (Speaking in overly dull voice), Drink the new punch! It tastes great and is made from the best stuff on earth, stuff like used dishwater, beaver sweat….."(The Director interrupts)
Director: Cut! That sounded like you don't like the stuff! Sound sincere! Okay! Let's try it again!
Cameraman: But Miss!
Director: No buts! Action!

(The Actor begins again this time with the appropriate level of sincerity. The interruptions by the director and cameraman continue, with the director saying things like it's too fast, too slow, until finally, everything goes smoothly. While the Cameraman keeps on saying but Miss, or there is something I need to tell you, with the director cutting the cameraman off each time)

Director: Cut! And print! That was fantastic! Let's get out of here!
Cameraman: But Miss! We don't have any film!
Optionally, the director can chase the cameraman off.

Emergency Broadcast System

Participants: 4 to 10
Props: None

A group of girls gather in front of the audience. On queue everyone in the group hums in a high pitched tone, very similar to what you might hear on the radio during an emergency broadcast system alert. After a about 20 seconds the humming stops and an MC or girl from the group comes forward and says, "This has been a test of the Charter _____ Emergency Broadcast System. This was only a test. If this had been an actual emergency, what you would hear would sound like this." Immediately following this speech all the girls in the group begin screaming and running in all different directions in what appears to be a terrified panic.

The Human Xylophone

Participants: 5 or more
Props: None

The skit is performed by a skit leader who states that she is going to play a song on a human xylophone. Several girls kneel in a line at the front of the campfire. Each is assigned the part of a musical note. They are told to speak or hum a musical key whenever they are touched on the head. They can all say the word "La" or each can be assigned a different word like "do, re, mi, fa, so, la, ti,). Simple songs such as "Twinkle, Twinkle Little Star," can be played out this way. Regardless of the song performed, this skit requires thorough practice.

Variation 1: A conductor can be added to lead this team. girls can be instructed to sing their note in a higher or lower pitch based on how high or low the conductor raised her hand. The conductor can provide additional comedy to this sketch by raising her arm higher and higher or by placing her hand near the ground for girls to try and hit impossibly low notes. Optionally, the conductor can cover her ears, or turn away from performers who sing off key.

The Crying Skit

Participants: 4 to 5
Props: Handkerchiefs

A girl comes on stage crying. A second girl comes out and asks the first girl what's wrong. The first girl whispers in the second girl's ear and they both start crying, long and loud. Several others come out one at a time, and repeat the same action. When everyone is on stage, crying, moaning, howling, sniffing and so on (using large handkerchiefs that were dipped in water before their entrance and wringing them out splashily,) the last participant comes out and asks aloud: "Why is everyone crying?" They all answer in unison: "Because we haven't got a skit!"

The Viper

Participants: 3 or more
Props: (optional) Squeegee and sponge or toilet paper

This skit has many variations. Here are two....

A girl runs to the front of the campfire and informs the leader that she has just received a message that the Viper is coming. The Leader gets very agitated and upset repeating the girl's message. Several others come in repeating the same message. They are all in a state of panic when the last person comes on stage with a squeegee and a sponge announcing, "I'm the vindow viper. I've come to vipe your vindows. Vhere do I start?"

Variation
Four girls run out in succession. The first says something like "here comes the viper, hide". girls 2, 3 and 4 make similar comments. The final girl ends the skit with the following punch-line, "Hi I'm the viper. (optionally holding out the roll of toilet paper) Does anyone need viping?"

Forty-Nine

Participants: 2
Props: Garbage can lid or cardboard cut-out to simulate a man-hole cover

A girl is jumping on up and down, yelling 49! 49! 49! The second girl comes by and notices this; she asks what she is doing.

Victim: What are you doing?
Jumper: I'm jumping up and down on this manhole yelling 49! 49! 49! It's really fun! Wanna try?
Victim: Sure!

She takes the jumper's place and yells 49! 49! 49! All of a sudden, the jumper pulls the manhole cover out from under the victim, who pretends to fall into the sewer. The jumper replaces the lid and begins again....
Jumper: 50! 50! 50!

The Poison Spring

Participants: 4 or more
Props: 2 or 3 ladles, 1 bucket, rice or confetti

One by one the participants drag themselves on stage crying for water. Each reaches a bucket with a ladle and takes a drink, splashing some water to show there is really water in it and dies. Generally, girls get a good audience reaction by "hamming up" the death scene. More than a ladle will probably be needed so that there is plenty of water to slosh around. The next to the last person starts to drink from the bucket, when the final person comes in. Seeing all the dead bodies, the last person yells, "Don't drink from that bucket, the water has been poisoned." Then the last person runs on stage, grabs the bucket and throws it on the audience. Of course, other than the water that was in the ladles the bucket is empty or contains something harmless like rice or confetti.

The Lost Quarter

Participants: 5 minimum
Props: Sleeping bags

Scene: One person acts as a lamppost, shining a flashlight on the ground. Another is groping around in the pool of light. (He's girl 1). girl 3 enters, sees girl 1, and begins the dialog:

Girl 3: What are you looking for?
Girl 1: A quarter that I lost.

Girl 3 joins girl 1, and helps her search. Other girls enter and repeat the above scene. Finally the last girl to enter turns to girl 1 and asks:
Last girl: Where did you lose the quarter?
Girl 1: (Pointing away) Over there.
Last girl: Then why are you looking here?"
Girl 1: Because the light is better over here!

The Factory Guard

Participants: 4 or 5
Props: Empty cardboard boxes

Manager: (To new guard) I'm giving you the very responsible position of gate guard at this factory. Because of the lack of vigilance by your predecessors, the workers have stolen so many finished articles that the firm is heading for bankruptcy. Your duty is to ensure this is brought to an end. Do you understand?
Guard: Yes, Mam. I am to stop stealing.
Manager: That's right. You can search workers if necessary. Now it's up to you, and let's see some results.
Guard: Very good, Mam. (Manager leaves; guard takes post; first workman enters carrying a box with a blanket draped over it.) Just a moment. What have you got in that box?
Employee 1: What do you mean?
Guard: What have you got in that box? It's my duty to see that no one takes stuff out of the factory.
Employee 1: Why didn't you say? There's nothing in the box. Look! (He shows everyone the box is empty.)
Guard: Oh, well, that's all right then.

(#1 leaves and #2 enters, box draped as before. Guard and workman go through routine of looking in the box. Repeat with #3. After #3 has left, the manager races in enraged.)

Manager: What's the matter with you? I hired you to stop this pilfering. You've only been here half an hour and already we're losing things!
Guard: But the only people who went out were three men with boxes. I stopped them all and they all had nothing in them.
Manager: We make boxes!

Scientific Genius

Participants: 3 or more
Props: Rocket ship (cardboard cutout)

The announcer tells the audience they are at the scene of a secret governmental test site where a highly classified rocket is to be launched by America's leading scientists. A rocket and or launching pad cut out of cardboard can be used as a prop in this skit. After an elaborate countdown, the rocket fails to launch at zero. After unexpected gasps and questions about what could possibly have gone wrong, those present inspect it. Using highly scientific sounding terms, the participants examine a number of highly scientific sounding devices - the supersonic sector compressor; the thermonuclear 0-rings, the trimeric rocket fuel igniters, etc. All seem perfect. Finally, a young girl walks out of the audience and says, "I think I see the problem. Someone forgot to put fuel in the rocket.... "

Animal Impressions

Participants: 3 or 4
Props: None

The announcer selects volunteers who come forward. These volunteers are told they can win prizes if they can get an audience member to successfully guess what animal sound or call they have been instructed to make. The announcer then whispers in the volunteer's ear, or alternatively hands the volunteer a piece of paper, indicating what animal call the volunteer is to make. Early volunteers are given animals that are easy to imitate, like a cow (the volunteer says "moo"), horse ("neigh"), or sheep ("baa"). Each volunteer is heartily congratulated on a job well done as the audience successfully identifies their animal call; these volunteers are then awarded prizes (real or imaginary). The final volunteer ("the victim") is then selected. Try to choose an adult leader or an older girl with a good sense of humor. This volunteer is told to make the call of some animals that the audience will not be able to guess. This can be animals that no one has ever heard of like the fissiroal bill goatsucker, muskox, african jerboa, pangolin (an asian anteater), wombat, etc. or you can choose animals that make little or no sound like rabbits, deer, or skunks. As the audience is unable to identify each animal the announcer says, "Oh, I'm sorry the audience just can't seem to identify your impression. Let's give our volunteer another try." The volunteer is then given the name of another animal that is impossible to imitate.

There are various options that can be used to end this skit. Generally the skit ends after the audience is unable to guess the victim's third animal impression. This can simply be an impossible animal to impersonate or it can be a Wild Boar or Old Goat. The skit then ends when the announcer says, "For those of you who were unable to guess, our volunteer is a …..(Wild Boar or Old Goat etc)."

Printed in Great Britain
by Amazon